Deluxe Edition
George Shearing
Interpretations For Piano

Copyright © 1994 CPP/Belwin, Inc.
15800 N.W. 48th Avenue, Miami, Florida 33014

Photography: Christian Steiner
Layout: Leyla Arner / Editor: David C. Olsen

ISBN 0-89898-470-X

9 780898 984705

THE EPITOME OF
SOPHISTICATED JAZZ:
THE SHEARING SOUND.

URBANE, CLEVER,
CHARMING:
**THE SHEARING
PERSONALITY.**

VERSATILE,
DYNAMIC, SENSITIVE:
THE SHEARING GENIUS.

London-born George Shearing has created an international reputation for his musical talent as pianist, arranger, and composer. Equally at home on the classical concert stage as on the jazz nightclub stand, consistently compelling with quintet, trio, duo, full orchestra or in solo performance, Shearing is recognized for his inventive, orchestrated jazz.

Offstage as well, Shearing is a dedicated musician. His compositions number more than one hundred, including his famous "Lullaby of Birdland," which has become a jazz standard. His latest publications are a series of original works dedicated to other great jazz pianists. As an educator, he has devoted many summers to teaching jazz technique, arrangement, and ensemble playing at the Aspen Summer Music Festival, the famed University of Utah Jazz Workshop, and the renowned Chautauqua Institution. As a student, George studies classical styles — Mozart and Bach are favorites.

IN THE BEGINNING ...

George Albert Shearing was born on August 13, 1919 in the Battersea area of London. Congenitally blind, he was the youngest of nine children. George discovered his musical talent when he found he could duplicate on the piano the tunes he heard on the family crystal set. His only formal musical education consisted of four years of study at the Linden Lodge School for the Blind. While his talent won him a number of university scholarships, he was forced to refuse them in favor of a more lucrative pursuit: playing piano in a neighborhood pub. After a series of similar club dates, George joined an all-blind band in the 1930s, a short-lived project sponsored by the Royal National Institution for the Blind. At this point, George developed a friendship with the noted jazz critic, Leonard Feather, and through this contact he made his first appearance on BBC radio. He also cut his first record, "Squeezing the Blues," playing accordion to Feather's piano accompaniment.

Shearing's keyboard reputation flourished through engagements in top London supper clubs and as a frequent guest on the BBC. While still in his twenties, he landed a recording contract with Decca Records and became one of the top-selling artists in Britain. In 1941, George won his first popularity poll victory in The Melody Maker *magazine; for the next seven years, he dominated British jazz polls. Also in 1941, he married Trixie Bayes whom he met while playing to huddled Londoners in an air raid shelter during a bombing blitz.*

In 1947, the Shearings and their five-year-old daughter, Wendy, moved to America where George spent two long years reestablishing his fame on this side of the Atlantic. The Shearing sound commanded national attention when, in 1949 he gathered a quintet, featuring his distinctive blend of piano, bass, drums, guitar and vibes to record "September in the Rain" for M.G.M. The record was an overnight success. His U.S. reputation was permanently entrenched when he was booked into New York's Birdland, to which he later penned his "Lullaby." Since then one of the country's most consistent sellers, George recorded for M.G.M. until 1955 when he signed with Capitol. Among his favorite albums from this period are those recorded with the late Nat "King" Cole, Peggy Lee, Wes Montgomery and Nancy Wilson (whom George introduced to the record industry).

But Shearing is very much a part of the present, still evolving, still experimenting. In 1978, he abandoned the quintet format to work as a duo with a bassist. "The idea of a duo appealed to me. I can get a lot of inner voices, I'm not tied down or congested by any group sounds. This is the real milieu I want to work in," says George. The Duo is currently available on the Concord lable. And — Shearing sings these days: warm, melting ballads where George allows the lyrics to breathe in his elegant, unrushed style; and in clubs and concert halls, deliciously witty parodies peppered with perfectly-timed, mischievous pauses.

Over the last two decades, George has been able to indulge his passion for classical music by often including a concerto on his symphony concerts. Engagements with such major orchestras as Cleveland, the Boston Pops, the Los Angeles Philharmonic, Detroit, Atlanta, Houston, the Pittsburgh Pops, Milwaukee, Portland, Buffalo, Utah, St. Louis, Minneapolis, Denver, Baltimore, Nashville, Chattanooga, Cincinnati and Tulsa have brought him under the batons of Louis Lane, John Williams, Peter Nero, Maurice Abravanelle, Leonard Slatkin, Arthur Fiedler, Erich Kunzel and others.

Since 1974 alone, George Shearing has travelled to Japan, Brazil, South Africa, the West Indies, Australia, and fifteen European countries to share his music. Most recently, such touring has included six consecutive concerts at the Royal Festival Hall in London, enabling him to maintain his ties with the still-loyal fans of his birthplace. In this country, he has performed more than 400 concerts in cities across the nation and appeared at some of the finest clubs and hotels. He has played concerts at the Hollywood Bowl, the Kennedy Center and Carnegie Hall, and appeared on major U.S. Jazz Festivals (Paul Masson, Kool Jazz, Aspen, Wolf Trap, Concorde, Ravinia, Etc.).

George has accumulated awards from every trade journal and jazz poll, including seven citations from Down Beat Magazine. In the fall of 1980, Billboard listed Shearing among the top forty albums in both the Classical and Jazz categories! And the two Concord discs with Mel Torme, recorded in 1982 and 1983, have both been Grammy Award winners. On the personal side, George received an honorary Doctor of Music degree from Westminster College, Salt Lake City, Utah in 1975 and the prestigious Horatio Alger Award in 1978 at a ceremony at New York's Waldorf Astoria Hotel. And The Shearing Center, a community recreational facility, opened recently in Battersea, the section of London where George was born.

Three Presidents have invited Shearing to play at the White House. In August, 1976, one of the thrills of George's career came when he performed after a State Dinner honoring president Kekkonen of Finland. Afterward he received a letter of thanks in braille from President and Mrs. Ford. He returned during the Carter Administration to play an all-Gershwin program for Romanian President Ceausescu and again in April, 1982 to play for Queen Beatrix and Prince Claus of the Netherlands as the guest of President and Mrs. Reagan.

Another aspect of Shearing's performance career is the concerts he frequently plays for favorite charities: The Hadley School for the Blind in Chicago (where he completed a correspondence course in business law); the Guide Dog Facility in San Rafael, California, where his own dog Leland (now deceased) was trained; the Lupus Foundation; and the Jewish Guild for the Blind in New York City. In January of 1982, George joined Frank Sinatra and Luciano Pavarotti at Radio City Music Hall, and before a sold out house, raised two million dollars for the Sloan Kettering Cancer Center in New York.

Music is his business, but there are other dimensions to George Shearing's life. During the rare weeks he takes a vacation between engagements, George relaxes in his Manhattan residence with second wife, Ellie Geffert, a mezzo-soprano, former teacher, and gourmet cook. It is Ellie who provides the orchestral part on the twin practice piano when George is working on a concerto. In March, 1980, George and Ellie were featured in a CBS News Profile and have twice appeared on the PBS program, Over Easy. They were also the subjects of a People Magazine "Couples" article in September of 1979. Quite a pair!

A devoted father, a wicked bridge player, an aspiring chef, and a voracious reader of (literally!) anything he can get this hands on. Shearing the talent. Shearing the man. All with the touch of genius!

TABLE OF CONTENTS

LULLABY OF BIRDLAND

By GEORGE SHEARING

Moderately

Lullaby Of Birdland - 3 - 1

From the 20th Century-Fox CinemaScope Production "AN AFFAIR TO REMEMBER"

AN AFFAIR TO REMEMBER

(OUR LOVE AFFAIR)

HAROLD ADAMSON
LEO McCAREY
HARRY WARREN

Moderately

An Affair To Remember - 2 - 1

An Affair To Remember - 2 - 2

ALL TOO SOON

CARL SIGMAN
DUKE ELLINGTON

Slowly (*with expression*)

All Too Soon - 2 - 2

From the 20th Century-Fox CinemaScope Production "APRIL LOVE"

APRIL LOVE

PAUL FRANCIS WEBSTER
SAMMY FAIN

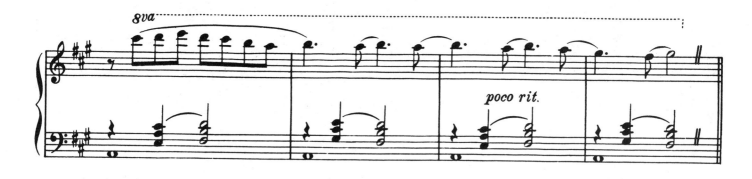

April Love - 2 - 1

BLUE MOON

LORENZ HART
RICHARD RODGERS

Moderately with feeling

Blue Moon - 2 - 1

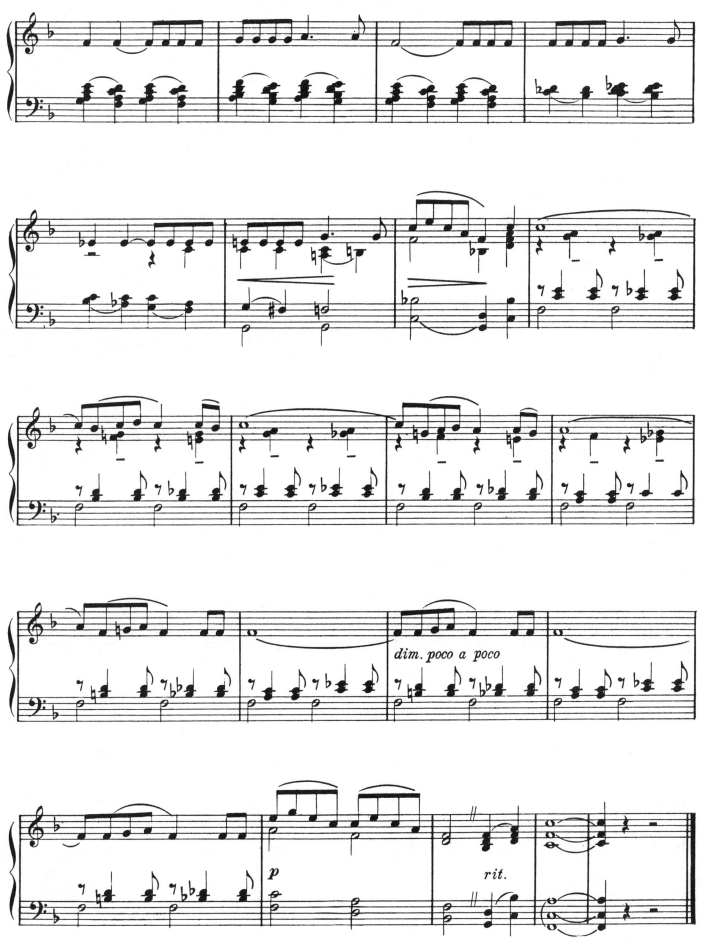

From the Albert Lewis-Vinton Freedley Musical Play "CABIN IN THE SKY"

CABIN IN THE SKY

By JOHN LATOUCHE
and VERNON DUKE

Cabin In The Sky - 2 - 1

cresc. e accel.

f

p subito rit.

From the 20th Century-Fox CinemaScope Production "A CERTAIN SMILE"

A CERTAIN SMILE

By PAUL FRANCIS WEBSTER
and SAMMY FAIN

Quietly with expression

A Certain Smile - 2 - 1

poco cresc.

rit. e dim.

p

COQUETTE

GUS KAHN
CARMEN LOMBARDO
JOHNNY GREEN

Slow Bounce

Coquette - 2 - 1

Coquette - 2 - 2

From the M-G-M Motion Picture "SWEET BIRD OF YO

EBB TIDE

CARL SIGMAN
ROBERT MAXWELL

Ebb Tide - 3 - 1

Ebb Tide - 3 - 2

From the M-G-M Motion Picture "GREEN DOLPHIN STREET"

ON GREEN DOLPHIN STREET

NED WASHINGTON
BRONISLAU KAPER

On Green Dolphin Street - 3 - 1

FOR ALL WE KNOW

SAM M. LEWIS
J. FRED COOTS

For All We Know - 2 - 1

For All We Know - 2 - 2

From William Wyler's "FRIENDLY PERSUASION". An Allied Artists Picture.

FRIENDLY PERSUASION

(Thee I Love)

PAUL FRANCIS WEBSTER
DIMITRI TIOMKIN

Friendly Persuasion - 2 - 1

HOW ABOUT YOU

RALPH FREED
BURTON LANE

Moderately

How About You - 2 - 1

How About You - 2 - 2

HOW AM I TO KNOW?

DOROTHY PARKER
JACK KING

Moderately

How Am I To Know? - 2 - 1

p subito

I GOT IT BAD AND THAT AIN'T GOOD

PAUL FRANCIS WEBSTER
DUKE ELLINGTON

Moderately Slow

I Got It Bad And That Ain't Good - 2 - 1

I Got It Bad And That Ain't Good - 2 - 2

ALL I DO IS DREAM OF YOU

Piano Interpretation by
GEORGE SHEARING

ARTHUR FREED
NACIO HERB BROWN

SWEET AND LOVELY

Piano Interpretation by
GEORGE SHEARING

GUS ARNHEIM
HARRY TOBIAS
JULES LEMARE

I'M IN THE MOOD FOR LOVE

JIMMY McHUGH
DOROTHY FIELDS

I'm In The Mood For Love - 2 - 1

I'm In The Mood For Love - 2 - 2

IF I GIVE MY HEART TO YOU

Words and Music by
JIMMIE CRANE, AL JACOBS
and JIMMY BREWSTER

Slowly

If I Give My Heart To You - 2 - 1

If I Give My Heart To You - 2 - 2

Based on the Theme of the M-G-M Motion Picture "INVITATION"

INVITATION

PAUL FRANCIS WEBSTER
BRONISLAU KAPER

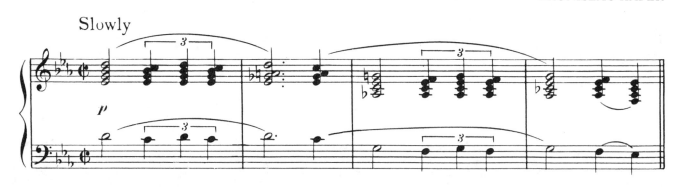

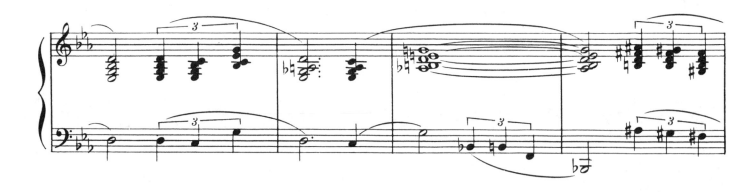

Invitation - 3 - 1

From the M-G-M Motion Picture "THE SANDPIPER"

THE SHADOW OF YOUR SMILE
(Love Theme From "THE SANDPIPER")

PAUL FRANCIS WEBSTER
JOHNNY MANDEL

Slowly, with expression

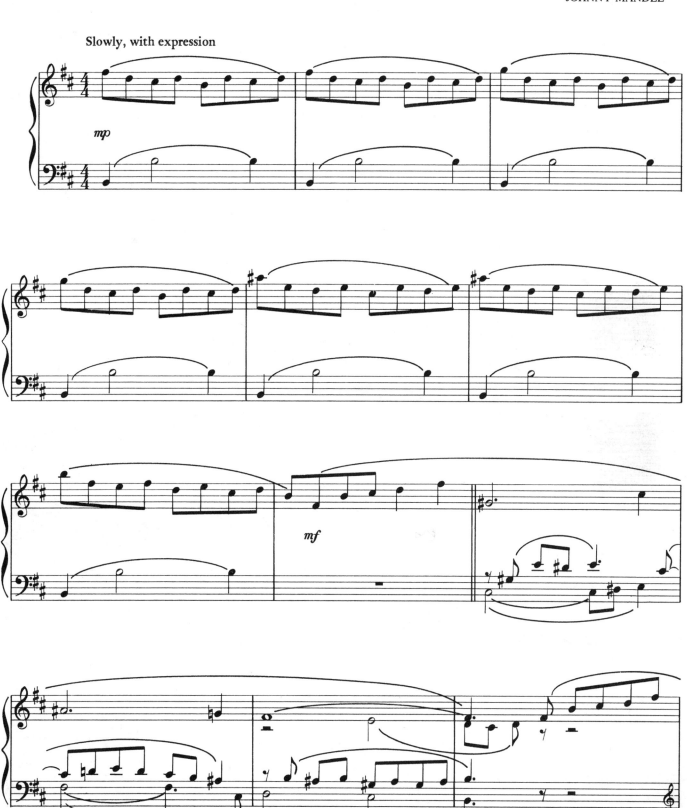

The Shadow Of Your Smile - 3 - 1

The Shadow Of Your Smile - 3 - 2

dim. poco a poco

p

The Shadow Of Your Smile - 3 - 3

JUST YOU, JUST ME

By RAYMOND KLAGES
and JESSE GREER

Brightly with a beat

Just You, Just Me - 2 - 1

Just You, Just Me - 2 - 2

Theme Melody from the 20th Century-Fox Picture "LAURA"

LAURA

JOHNNY MERCER
DAVID RAKSIN

Laura - 2 - 1

From the 20th Century-Fox Motion Picture "LOVE IS A MANY-SPLENDORED THING"

LOVE IS A MANY-SPLENDORED THING

PAUL FRANCIS WEBSTER
SAMMY FAIN

Love Is A Many-Splendored Thing - 2 - 2

Recorded by BOBBY VINTON on ABC Records

MOONLIGHT SERENADE

Piano Interpretation by
GEORGE SHEARING

MITCHELL PARISH
GLENN MILLER

Tempo I

Theme from the 20TH CENTURY-FOX Motion Picture "THREE COINS IN THE FOUNTAIN"

THREE COINS IN THE FOUNTAIN

Piano Interpretation by
GEORGE SHEARING

SAMMY CAHN
JULE STYNE

SHOULD I

ARTHUR FREED
NACIO HERB BROWN

Brightly

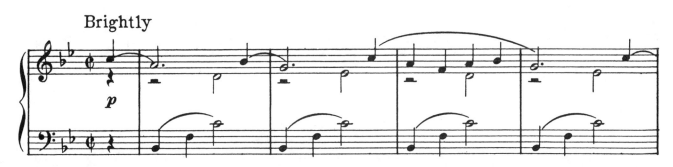

Should I - 3 - 1

66

Should I - 3 - 2

Recorded by CARLY SIMON on ELEKTRA Records
From the United Artists Motion Picture "THE SPY WHO LOVED ME"

NOBODY DOES IT BETTER

CAROLE BAYER SAGER
MARVIN HAMLISCH

Moderately slow (smooth and rhythmic)

Nobody Does It Better - 4 - 1

ONCE IN A WHILE

BUD GREEN
MICHAEL EDWARDS

Once In A While - 2 - 1

Once In A While - 2 - 2

From the M-G-M Motion Picture "THE WIZARD OF OZ"

OVER THE RAINBOW

E.Y. HARBURG
HAROLD ARLEN

Over The Rainbow - 2 - 1

From the 20th Century Fox Motion Picture "THE SECOND TIME AROUND"

THE SECOND TIME AROUND

SAMMY CAHN
JAMES VAN HEUSEN

Moderately slow

The Second Time Around - 2 - 1

Featured in Dwight Deere Wiman's Musical Comedy "I MARRIED AN ANGEL"

SPRING IS HERE

LORENZ HART
RICHARD RODGERS

STREET OF DREAMS

SAM M. LEWIS
VICTOR YOUNG

Street Of Dreams - 2 - 1

Street Of Dreams - 2 - 2

SUNDAY

By NED MILLER, CHESTER CONN,
JULES STEIN and BENNIE KRUEGER

Moderately with a beat

Sunday - 2 - 1

TAKING A CHANCE ON LOVE

JOHN LATOUCHE
TED FETTER
VERNON DUKE

Moderately

Taking A Chance On Love - 2 - 1

Taking A Chance On Love - 2 - 2

From the 20th Century-Fox CinemaScope Production "TENDER IS THE NIGHT"

TENDER IS THE NIGHT

By PAUL FRANCIS WEBSTER
and SAMMY FAIN

Tender Is The Night - 2 - 1

THAT OLD FEELING

LEW BROWN
SAMMY FAIN

That Old Feeling - 2 - 1

That Old Feeling - 2 - 2

From the United Artists Motion Picture "THE HAPPY ENDING"

WHAT ARE YOU DOING THE REST OF YOUR LIFE?

ALAN and MARILYN BERGMAN
MICHEL LEGRAND

Slowly (freely, with expression)

What Are You Doing The Rest Of Your Life? - 3 - 1

What Are You Doing The Rest Of Your Life? - 3 - 2

92

What Are You Doing The Rest Of Your Life? - 3 - 3

From the M-G-M Motion Picture "GOING HOLLYWOOD"

TEMPTATION

ARTHUR FREED
NACIO HERB BROWN

Temptation - 3 - 1

94

Temptation - 3 - 2

Temptation - 3 - 3

DISCOGRAPHY

CAPITOL

THE SHEARING SPELL
VELVET CARPET
LATIN ESCAPADE
BLACK SATIN
SHEARING PIANO
NIGHT MIST
IN THE NIGHT
BURNISHED BRASS
LATIN LACE
BLUE CHIFFON
ON STAGE
LATIN AFFAIR
SATIN BRASS
WHITE SATIN
SUNNY SIDE OF THE STRIP
SHEARING TOUCH
SWINGING'S MUTUAL
MOOD LATINO
NAT "KING" COLE SINGS,
  GEORGE SHEARING PLAYS
CONCERTO FOR MY LOVE
SAN FRANCISCO SCENE
BOSSA NOVE
JAZZ MOMENTS
OLD GOLD AND IVORY
TOUCH ME SOFTLY
DEEP VELVET
OUT OF THE WOODS
LATIN RENDEVOUS
HERE AND NOW
RARE FORM
NEW LOOK
BEAUTY AND THE BEAT
JAZZ CONCERT
SATIN AFFAIR
SHEARING TODAY
THAT FRESH FEELING
THE FOOL ON THE HILL

CONCORD JAZZ

BLUES ALLEY JAZZ (Duo, 2/80)
TWO FOR THE ROAD - CARMEN McRAE
  AND GEORGE SHEARING (8/80)
ON A CLEAR DAY (Duo, 10/80)
ALONE TOGETHER - MARIAN McPARTLAND
  AND GEORGE SHEARING (10/81)

SHEBA

HEART AND SOUL OF JOE WILLIAMS
  AND GEORGE SHEARING (1971)

GEORGE SHEARING OUT OF THIS WORLD
  Piano Solo (1971)

GEORGE SHEARING TRIO #1 (1971)

GEORGE SHEARING QUARTET (1972)

AS REQUESTED: SHEARING QUINTET (1972)

MUSIC TO HEAR: Piano Solo (1973)

MPS

GEORGE SHEARING: LIGHT, AIRY AND
  SWINGING (Trio) (1973)

THE WAY WE ARE — THE GEORGE SHEARING
  QUINTET + AMIGOS (1974)

CONTINENTAL EXPERIENCE — THE
  GEORGE SHEARING QUINTET
  + AMIGOS (1975)

MY SHIP Piano Solo (1976)

REUNION Shearing Trio with Stefan Grappelli
  (1978)

GETTING IN THE SWING OF THINGS Trio with Stewart,
  Orsted-Pederson (1979)

ANGEL

CONCERTO FOR CLASSIC GUITAR &
  JAZZ PIANO by Bolling, with Romero,
  Manne & Brown (1980)

FIRST EDITION (with Jim Hall, 3/82)

AN EVENING WITH GEORGE SHEARING
  AND MEL TORME (9/82)*

TOP DRAWER (Duo with Torme, 7/83)*

*Grammy Winners